CANADA

A PICTURE BOOK TO REMEMBER HER BY

Designed by
DAVID GIBBON

Produced by
TED SMART

CRESCENT

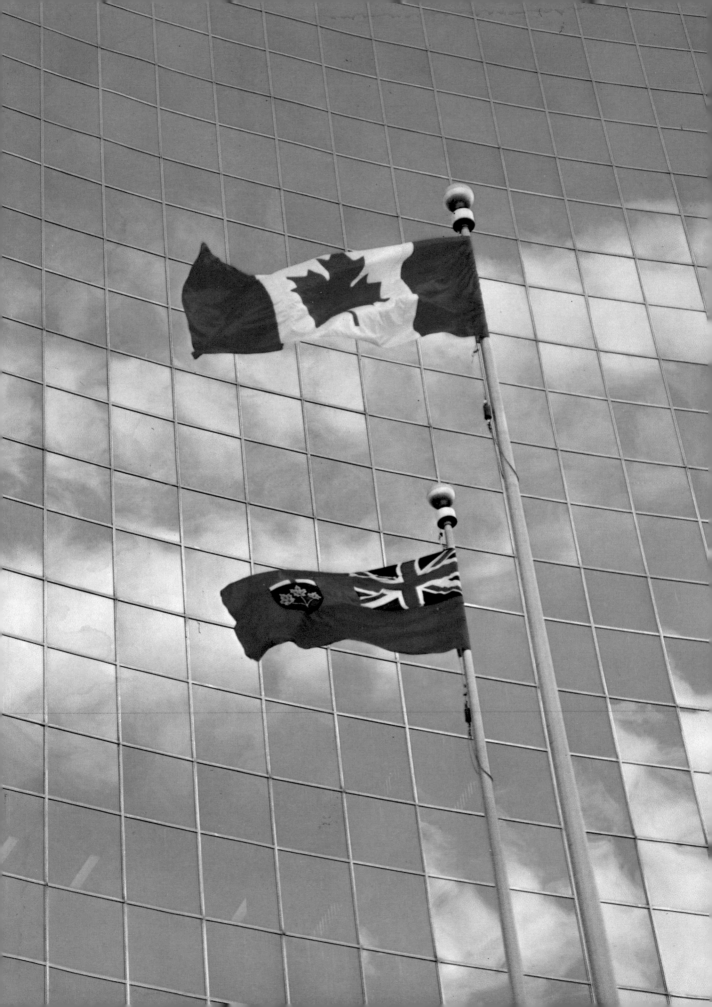

INTRODUCTION

One of the most striking features of Canada is its tremendous size. After the USSR and China it is the third largest country in the world but, unlike the other two, Canada has a very small population, numbering less than twenty millions.

Settlement began in 1604 when the French explorer Samuel de Champlain, together with seventy-nine settlers, wintered on Sainte Croix Island. Only forty-four survived until the spring but it was these survivors, four years later, who founded the present city of Quebec.

In 1609 sixty-two English settlers made permanent homes on Newfoundland, attracted by the rich cod fishing that was to be found around the island.

When the first population census was taken in 1666 it showed 3,215 inhabitants but this, of course, did not include the indigenous population of Red Indians or Eskimos. Since that time the peaks of growth have coincided with the American Revolution, the Irish Famine, the building of the Canadian railways and the opening up of the West.

Canada's economic growth has been strongly connected with fish, fur, timber, farming, manufacturing and, more recently, oil and natural gas. The fur trade began when French fishermen came into contact with bands of hunting Indians along the St. Lawrence River. During the 17th century the Indian's demand for gunpowder and iron goods, together with the spread of the beaver hat as a fashion in Europe, brought rapid expansion to this new trade and it continued to flourish for some 300 years. Nowadays it has greatly declined and although in the Northwest Territories and the Yukon one million square miles is reserved for native trappers, much of Canada's fur trade is through licensed fur farms.

The Napoleonic Wars and Britain's need for ship building timber created the next major economic development. Nearly half of Canada is forested with trees such as giant red cedars, Douglas firs and redwoods and she is therefore able to meet the large demands for timber from other countries. Today there are numerous pulp, paper and saw mills throughout the country and the Canadians exercise great care in the replanting of their valuable natural resources.

It was the early, timber carrying ships that returned from Europe with large numbers of immigrants, and it was these new Canadians who were responsible for opening up new land for farming. Much of the land was in central Canada, in the region known as the Prairies. When they arrived there the settlers found vast grasslands stretching as far as the eye could see. There were no roads and no buildings, only large herds of buffalo and a few Red Indian tribes. At first the newcomers kept cattle but, with the building of the railways and the introduction of the steel plough, the grass was ripped up and the grain was planted to satisfy the demand for wheat in Europe. The Royal Canadian Mounted police were established in 1873 for the purpose of maintaining law and order in the Western Prairies, to safeguard the building of the railways and to protect the new settlers. The now famous scarlet jackets of the R.C.M.P. were adopted as part of their uniform because the Red Indians had trusted the red-clad British soldiers.

The construction of the railways was a tremendous step forward in the economic growth of Canada. The privately owned Canadian Pacific Railway Company contracted to build a railway to connect the Atlantic and Pacific coasts. It was estimated that it would take ten years to complete but it was finished in less than five. In 1886 the first train left Montreal for Port Moody on the Pacific coast and the journey took over five days. Today the same journey takes three nights and the company now owns hotels, ocean liners and airways.

Canada's rivers and lakes were, of course, the first travel routes and they are remarkable for their number and size. The Great Lakes – St. Lawrence River system is now the principal waterway, navigable by ocean-going ships for 2,300 miles and it is of prime importance for the shipment of bulky freight such as iron ore, coal, oil, grain and timber.

For the tourist Canada is a paradise of open spaces with miles and miles of unspoiled countryside and scenery of every kind. It is also a modern, sophisticated country in which it is possible to combine the best of all worlds.

Left: Hydro Place, Ontario.

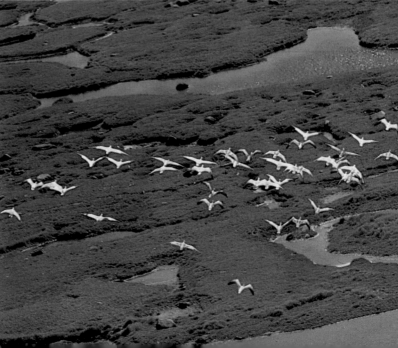

North of the prairie provinces of Alberta, Manitoba and Saskatchewan lie the Northwest Territories, a vast area that includes the islands of the Arctic Archipelago.

For man and beast alike, life is hard in this region of Canada, and an injured dog may find itself a passenger on a sled *above left,* during a hunting expedition.

There is a considerable variety of wildlife in the vast region of the Northwest Territories. An Eskimo hunter *far left* examines his latest kill – an Arctic Hare – and *left* Snow Geese fly above the tundra near the shore of Hudson Bay.

Living conditions are often primitive *top* and, during the winter months, communication with the outside world would be impossible if it were not for light aircraft *above.*

Although some areas of the Northwest Territories can be warm enough for the enjoyment of camping, sailing and fishing during the summer months, it is the harshness of the climate that is its most memorable feature. Frost and ice quickly form on hair and skin *right* and frostbite is almost certain unless adequate protective clothing is worn.

Travelling is a hazardous undertaking by any means of transport but Husky dogs seem able to cope with the conditions and they are still widely used *left and below*.

Newfoundland was once Britain's oldest colony. In 1949, however, it became the tenth, and youngest, province of Canada. Its capital is St. John's *below centre* and it is also the headquarters of the fishing industry in Newfoundland. Fishing forms a major part of the industry of the province and there are many fishing towns and villages along the coast, which are known as 'outports', such as Port-aux-Basques *right*. Fishermen *above* prepare codfish for drying in Port-de-Grave.

A sea of logs *far right, bottom* at St. John's.

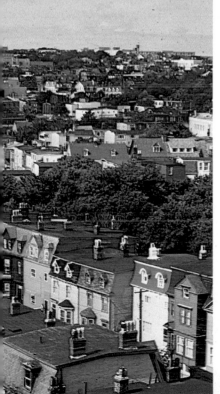
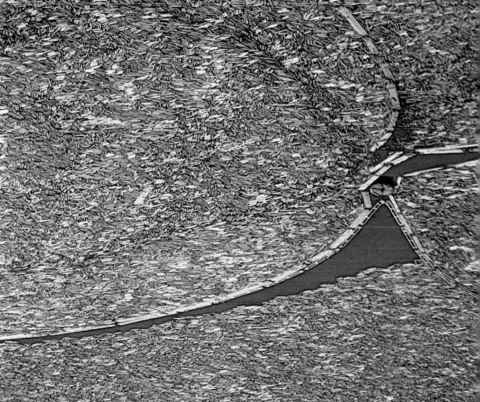

Nova Scotia is a maritime province consisting mainly of fertile uplands and valleys. It is a fortunate province in that it possesses great mineral wealth as well as valuable fisheries.

Part of the herring catch *top left* at Pubnico habour.

Nova Scotia is rich in coal and this has led to extensive industrialization such as the steel works *centre left* at Sydney.

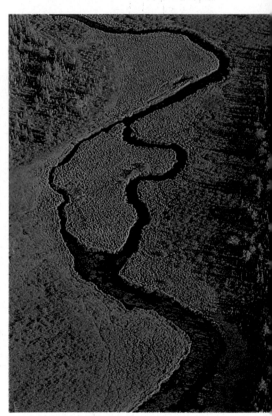

Much more recent than the utilization of the province's coal resources has been the discovery of, and drilling for *left*, off-shore oil.

Despite its industries, Nova Scotia still remains a beautiful province both in the interior as at Cape Breton *above* and along the coast, where there is a wealth of small fishing towns and villages like the picturesque Peggy's Cove *above right* and larger harbours and docks *right*.

The largest of Canada's provinces is Quebec. It occupies a huge area of the Labrador Peninsula on the eastern side of the country. The waters of Hudson Bay extend down its western coast to James Bay and its southern coastline is washed by the Gulf of St. Lawrence. Gaspé Peninsula *left and top far left* juts out into the Gulf. To the south of the Gaspé Peninsula, and still in the Gulf of St. Lawrence, lies Prince Edward Island *far left, centre and bottom,* which is known, because of the meeting there of the Fathers of Confederation in 1864, as the 'birthplace of Canada'. Bonaventure Island *below* is a favourite with visitors. The island is a wild bird refuge and, during the summer months, boats regularly carry trippers on tours.

Autumn colours *overleaf* reflected in a lake in Quebec Province.

Quebec City is the capital of the province of Quebec. It is a unique city in almost every way: a natural citadel that stands where the St. Lawrence River first narrows. Quebec City is almost entirely French-speaking and is primarily an administrative and cultural centre.

Château Frontenac, an internationally famous hotel *above* is a noted landmark.

The Quebec Government buildings *above left* are now dwarfed by tower blocks but, to offset this, there are still plenty of trees and open areas which provide a feeling of space.

Much restoration work has been carried out in the old sections of the city *left, far left and top.*

Greater Montreal has a population of nearly three million and it is the second largest French-speaking metropolis in the world and the largest inland seaport. It lies on an island and is connected to the mainland by a network of bridges and a tunnel.

These scenes in Montreal show: A general view of the city, the river and bridges *top left*, St. Joseph Oratorie *far left* and a night-time view from the 45th floor of the Canadian Imperial Banking building *centre left*, Dorchester Street and Dominion Square *left*, the Olympic Village *above* and the much-publicised Olympic Stadium *top*.

Mount Royal is a former volcano that rises some seven hundred feet above sea level and affords a splendid view across the city *overleaf*.

In 1857 an historic choice was made by Queen Victoria as to the choice of a permanent seat for the government of Canada. In the end Ottawa was chosen as it was said to "combine more advantages than any other place in Canada".

The construction of the three huge Victorian Gothic buildings *left and below* that house the government was commenced in 1859, and they still dominate the city from their setting on Parliament Hill. Changing the Guard *right* is a ceremony that takes place daily and it is an event that always draws crowds of visitors, particularly during the summer.

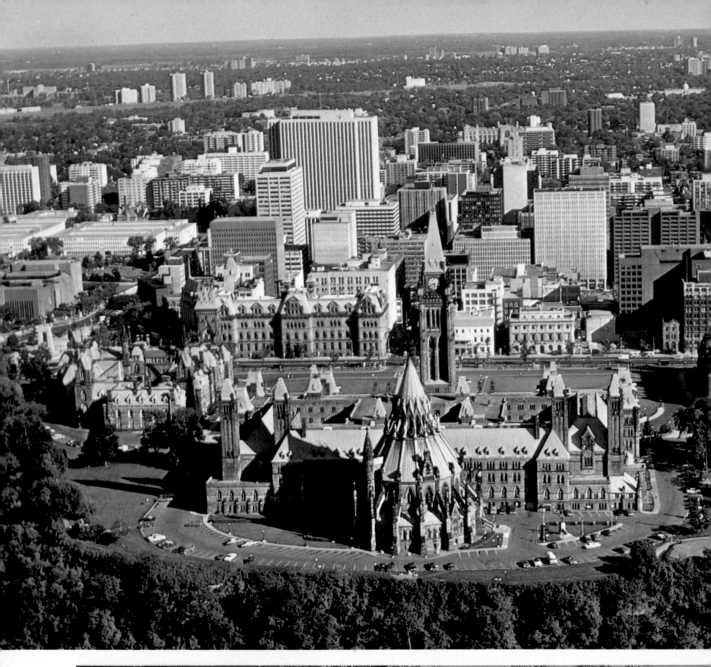

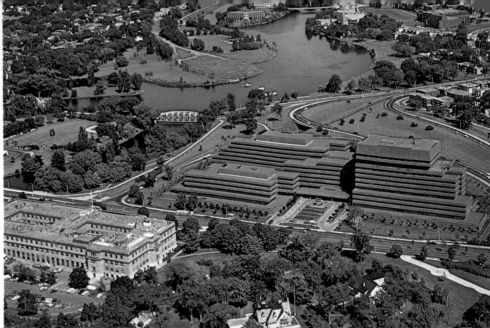

The old buildings of the Parliament are shown to advantage against some of the more modern towers and blocks *above left*, and framed by a tree in autumn leaf *far left*.

Rideau River *top* meanders its way around the island *above*, on which stands Ottawa City Hall, before literally falling into the Ottawa River at the Rideau Falls.

A bookseller, obviously keen to promote his country's own reading matter, in Confederation Square *left*.

A display of great natural beauty and immense power is provided by the spectacular Niagara Falls *right and below right*. The Canadian Horseshoe Falls are over 670 metres wide and 54 metres high. The falls have attracted many and varied visitors. Since early in the nineteenth century, stunt men have attempted to go over them in a variety of receptacles and wire-walkers have crossed them on tightropes. They have always exerted a fascination for tourists and, in particular, for honeymooners.

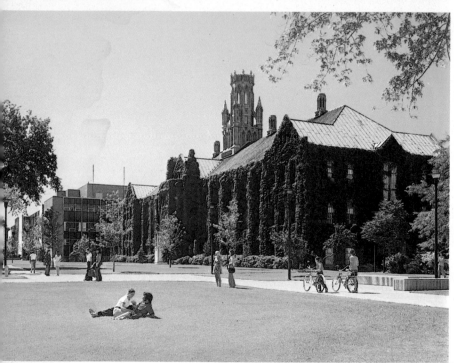

Flags fly in the breeze *top left* at Centennial Park, Windsor and the walls of the University of Windsor *centre left* are mellowed both by time and by their luxuriant covering of ivy.

Also in Windsor, Ontario, are the Dieppe Gardens *left* and the Windsor-Detroit riverfront *above*.

Kingston, Ontario, is situated at the eastern end of Lake Ontario, where the waters of the lake flow down the great St. Lawrence River, past Quebec, and on into the Gulf of St. Lawrence. *Below* is Kingston's City Hall, floodlit and with fountains playing, and *top left* is Belle View House.

The pictures on the *right* show the situation, colour and pageantry of Old Fort Henry which stands on a hill overlooking the city of Kingston. During summer, university students dress in nineteenth century uniforms and re-enact history for the pleasure of the thousands of visitors who come to see them.

The Soo Locks *left* at Sault Ste. Marie were constructed on St. Mary's River, between Lake Superior and Lake Huron in order to overcome the considerable difference in levels between the two lakes. The word *sault* is, in fact, an old French word which means "rapids".

Spanning the St. Lawrence River is the Thousand Islands International Bridge *centre left.* Thousand Islands is an area of Lake Huron *bottom left and right* dotted with small islands.

The rapids *above* are in Rushing River Provincial Park and the beautiful sunset *top right* was pictured at Old Millbay, Lake Superior.

Ontario's capital, Toronto, is dominated by the CN Tower *left and right* which at 533.33 metres is the tallest free-standing structure in the world. It provides facilities for the transmission of television and radio programmes and it boasts a revolving restaurant *below* as well as two observation decks with magnificent views across the city and beyond.

Standing high over Lake Ontario, on three man-made islands, Ontario Place *centre left, right and below right* provides a wide range of family entertainment. The world's largest curved cinema screen is housed in the domed cinesphere and in the rest of the complex there are excellent modern facilities for theatre and concert-going as well as for shopping and eating. There is also an extensive marina for those inclined towards sailing and boating.

The covered shopping area of Eaton Centre *above* was opened in 1977 and must rank as one of the finest in the world.

The floodlit sculpture *top left* is "The Archer" by Henry Moore and it stands in Nathan Phillips Square, isolated against a background of modern buildings which include City Hall *left*.

Toronto's impressive City Hall *left* consists of a white dome housed between two curved towers, one of twenty and the other of twenty-seven storeys. It was opened in 1965 and it is considered to have provided the impetus for the city's construction boom.

The Sheraton Centre and Toronto Hotel *bottom left* occupy the centre of the area pictured at night *centre left* which could hardly be more strongly contrasted than with Casa Loma *below*.

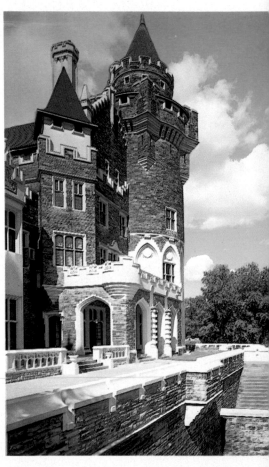

Despite its appearance, which suggests a medieval castle, Casa Loma was constructed between 1911 and 1914. Its builder, Sir Henry Pellatt, did, however, spend several years studying Old World Castles before constructing the building that has become a favourite amongst Toronto's many attractions.

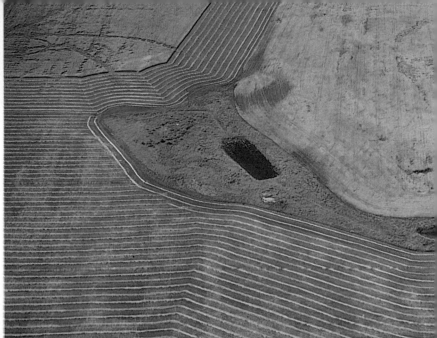

Manitoba is in the heartland of Canada. It is a province of lakes *bottom right* and rolling farmlands *top right,* grain elevators *left* and paddle steamers *below.*

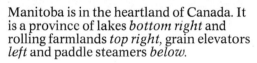

The capital of Manitoba is Winnipeg *above and right.* Winnipeg is a happy blend of the sophistication of the east of Canada and the rural friendliness of the west. The Manitoba Museum of Man is in Winnipeg and is certainly one of Canada's finest museums. The Manitoba Legislature *bottom left* is in classic Greek style and atop the dome is the famous Golden Boy, a gilded bronze statue of a running youth.

Saskatchewan is the major wheat-growing province of Canada and it stretches from the United States border right up to the Northwest Territories. In fact, until entering the Confederation in 1905, Saskatchewan formed part of the Northwest Territories. The province is one of wide horizons and under its broad skies are virgin grasslands, wilderness forests, rich grainfields, roaring waterfalls and busy cities.

Regina is the capital of Saskatchewan but it is for its "Big Sky Country" *these pages and overleaf* that the province is justly famed.

Edmonton, Alberta's capital and largest city, was chosen as the venue for the 1978 Commonwealth games. The city was already expanding fast but this news provided added impetus.

The city and its skyline *right, bottom left and below right* now seem to change from year to year. One such change was certainly provided by the sight of the pyramid-shaped structures of Muttart Conservatory *right* which was officially opened in 1976. Within the pyramids plants from arid, temperate and tropical regions are displayed.

Calgary *top left and centre left* was founded by the North West Mounted Police in 1875, at the confluence of the Bow and Elbow Rivers. The discovery of oil, virtually on the doorstep of the city, in 1914 was responsible, to a large extent, for the city's rapid growth and prosperity. Today it is Canada's major oil centre and the city houses the offices of more than 400 oil and petroleum related businesses. One of Calgary's major landmarks is the Calgary Tower *above*.

The Calgary Stampede is billed as "The Greatest Outdoor Show on Earth" and there are many thousands of people who would not argue with this description. The show is held in early July each year and it consists of ten days of sheer western excitement. The noise, dust, colour and general high spirits all add to the atmosphere of this great occasion and, as the organizers point out in their publicity handouts, it is a show in which the audience is invited, not just to watch, but to participate!

The 'Badlands' of Alberta provide some of the most spectacular scenery to be found in Canada. The names of some of the places can themselves conjure up all sorts of visions: Horse Thief Canyon, Dinosaur Valley and Writing-On-Stone Provincial Park amongst them.

The picture *left* shows the Red Deer River and Horse Thief Canyon and *below left* is Horse Thief Canyon again, but this time featuring the Dinosaur Trail.

HOODOOS

THESE STRANGE FORMATIONS ARE THE RESULT OF WIND & WATER EROSION. TWO DISTINCT FORMATIONS IN THE GEOLOGICAL HISTORY OF THE AREA ARE SHOWN ON THE HOODOO COLUMNS... THE BROWN OR BOTTOM LAYER IS THE BEARPAW FORMATION & WAS THE BOTTOM OF AN ANCIENT SEA SOME 75 MILLION YEARS AGO.... PETRIFIED MARINE LIFE IS FOUND HERE. THE TOP OR GREY PORTION OF THE HOODOOS IS PART OF THE EDMONTON FORMATION WHICH WAS A LATER PERIOD OF SWAMPY AND TROPICAL LIKE JUNGLE .... HERE THE DINOSAUR LIVED ......

The sign which is reproduced *top right* tells the story of the strange rock formations pictured *centre right* and *right*.

The Peace River area is known as one of the best farming areas in Alberta. The Indians called the river Unjigah, which means peace, from earliest times. It is a huge and beautiful river eminently suitable for canoeing although some of the falls *right* dictate a portage.

The Dunvegan Bridge *top left* provides access to the small township of Dunvegan. St. Charles Mission *centre left and bottom left* dates from the 1920's. It was restored during the 1950's and it has now been converted into a museum.

Columbia Icefield Snowmobile Tours Ltd. Jasper Alta.

A large area of the Canadian Rockies is covered by the Columbia Icefield. Twelve of the twenty-five highest mountains in this area are in the Icefield.

Athabasca Viewpoint *above* is a famous lookout along the Icefield Parkway. It opens up a vista towards the Athabasca River and the peaks of the Canadian Rockies.

The Jasper National Park *pictures this page* is rich in history. Along the Icefields Parkway, a 142 mile scenic route between Jasper and Lake Louise, the effect of glacier activity is everywhere in evidence and existing glaciers such as Stutfield and Dome Glaciers can also be seen.

A complete contrast to the rugged grandeur of the Rocky Mountains is provided by mile upon mile of grain, *right* waiting for the harvesters, after which it will be transported to grain stores such as these at Ponoka *above right*.

Vancouver is Canada's third largest city and is the business centre of British Columbia. It lies below the mountain playgrounds of Grouse, Hollyburn and Seymour and it is bounded to the north and west by Howe Sound and English Bay, and to the south and east by Fraser Valley and the Fraser Delta.

At the top of the page may be seen the lights of downtown Vancouver pictured from Stanley Park.

Two more views of Vancouver are shown *left and far left* and *above* is the H.R. MacMillan Planetarium and Centennial Museum of Natural History.

The new high-rise buildings of Vancouver's West End *right* are beautifully set off by the landscape of Vanier Park to the south of the city.

Top right and centre right are two vistas of the Queen Elizabeth Park Sunken Garden.

British Columbia is the most westerly of the Canadian provinces and it contains an incredible geographic variety. Within its boundaries, British Columbia has a dozen different mountain chains, four major river systems, many smaller rivers, countless lakes and a long and indented seacoast with attractive harbours *bottom left*.

One of British Columbia's major industries is logging. The picture *centre left* shows huge logs being loaded onto a transporter in the Bella Coola area and *overleaf* is a busy scene at a sawmill on the shore of Lake Slocan, near the city of Nelson.

Snow-capped mountains reflected in the water *above* at Peckham Lake, Norbury Provincial Park and *right* in the Robson River at Mount Robson National Park.

Victoria, the capital of British Columbia, is at
the southern end of Vancouver Island. It is a
truly beautiful city, much admired by such
famous writers as Rudyard Kipling who
compared it to some of the finest sights he
had seen in his travels.

The Provincial Government Building
above left faces directly onto the harbour
and the colourful yachts that throng it. *Top
right* is a general view of Victoria and the
inner harbour *centre right* with the impressive
Empress Hotel in the background, and a
seaplane *right* moored in the harbour.
Butchart's Gardens *left and far left* was once
a quarry which has now been transformed
into one of the world's most beautiful
gardens.

First published in Great Britain 1978 by Colour Library International Ltd.
© Illustrations: CLI/Bruce Coleman Ltd. Colour separations by La Cromolito, Milan, Italy.
Display and text filmsetting by Focus Photoset, London, England.
Printed and bound by L.E.G.O. Vicenza, Italy.
Published by Crescent Books, a division of Crown Publishers Inc.
All rights reserved.
Library of Congress Catalogue Card No. 77-18466
CRESCENT 1978